GRAPHIC FORENSIC SCIENCE

CORPSES AND SKELETONS:

THE SCIENCE OF FORENSIC ANTHROPOLOGY

by Rob Shone

illustrated by Nick Spender

FRANKLIN WATTS

LONDON • SYDNEY

First published in 2009 by Franklin Watts

Franklin Watts
338 Euston Road
London NW1 3BH

Franklin Watts Australia
Level 17/207 Kent Street
Sydney, NSW 2000

A CIP catalogue record for this book is available from the British Library.

Dewey number: 363.2'562

ISBN: 978 0 7496 9244 5

Franklin Watts is a division of Hachette Children's Books,
an Hachette UK company.
www.hachette.co.uk

GRAPHIC FORENSIC SCIENCE: CORPSES AND SKELETONS produced for
Franklin Watts by David West Children's Books, 7 Princeton Court,
55 Felsham Road, London SW15 1AZ

Designed and produced by
David West Children's Books

Editor: Gail Bushnell

Photo credits:
P4/5, istockphoto.com/Chris Ronneseth; 6t, U.S. National Library of Medicine; 6b,
istockphoto.com/Clayton Hansen; 7t, U.S. National Library of Medicine; 7b,
istockphoto.com/Jaroslaw Wojcik; 44t, istockphoto.com/Nikola Bilic; 45t,
istockphoto/Torbjorn Lagerwall.

Printed in China

Website disclaimer:
Note to parents and teachers: Every effort has been made by the Publishers to ensure
that the websites in this book are suitable for children, that they are of the highest
educational value, and that they contain no inappropriate or offensive material.
However, because of the nature of the Internet, it is impossible to guarantee that the
contents of these sites will not be altered. We strongly advise that the Internet is
supervised by a responsible adult.

CONTENTS

THE CRIME SCENE   4

BODIES, BUGS, AND BONES   6

THE GOUFFE CASE   8

BODY IN THE CARPET   24

THE CASKET MAN   32

OTHER FAMOUS CASES   44

GLOSSARY   46

FOR MORE INFORMATION   47

INDEX   48

THE CRIME SCENE

Human bones are often unearthed. They can be found on building sites, in ploughed fields and in fact anywhere the ground has been disturbed. Most are old and are of interest only to archaeologists. Some bones, however, belong to the victims of murder.

THE SIGNS OF MURDER

When a crime scene has been identified it is quickly made secure. Only a few people are allowed on to the scene, so evidence will not be damaged. Most of the evidence is collected by the crime scene investigators (CSI), or scene of crime officers (SOCO), as they are known in the UK. They make careful records of everything they see. The crime scene, and every piece of evidence, is photographed and drawn. Some forensic experts work alongside the CSI at this point. A forensic anthropologist will examine any bones that are found at the scene and later study them more closely in a laboratory. Another expert who might be there is the forensic entomologist. Insect samples would have to be collected from the scene as soon as possible.

The first thing
a forensic anthropologist
must do when examining bones is
to decide whether or not they are
human. Animal bones are quite
often mistaken for human ones.

BODIES, BUGS AND BONES

There are 206 bones in the human body. A forensic anthropologist must be able to recognise them all.

A dead body can turn into a skeleton in less than a month if the conditions are right. When a body has decomposed that much, normal detective work can be difficult. The police may have to rely on the experts for help.

FORENSIC ANTHROPOLOGY

Forensic anthropologists study the human skeleton. Their main job is to identify bodies. Just a few bones can tell them a great deal. A thigh bone or upper arm bone can give a height for the body. The thigh bone can also tell the anthropologist the sex of the skeleton, as can the skull, hip bone and teeth. These bones are different in men and women. As people grow older some of their bones change. This makes it possible to know the age of a skeleton. Forensic anthropologists also look for damage to bones. Marks made by knives, bullets or a blunt instrument can indicate how a person died. Signs of bone disease and bone wear might provide information about how a person lived.

The forensic anthropologist often works with a forensic odontologist (dentist). Using X-rays, they will try to match a skeleton to its dental records.

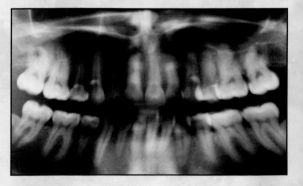

ART AND FORENSICS

While the forensic anthropologist can describe vital features such as the age of a skeleton when it was alive, the forensic artist can give the skeleton a face. This may help identify John and Jane Does (unidentified bodies). The forensic artist can also help solve cold cases, old crimes that are reexamined. The faces of people who have been missing for years can be drawn to show them looking older.

Knowing how the face muscles are arranged is vital if the forensic artist is to create a lifelike reconstruction.

Maggots may not be pretty to look at, but they are important to the forensic entomologist in finding a murder victim's time of death.

FORENSIC ENTOMOLOGY

Entomology is the study of insects. In criminal cases they are generally used to find the time of death of a murder victim. Many different types of insect will infest a dead body. They appear on the corpse in a particular order and after a set amount of time. Knowing this timetable allows the entomologist to work back and discover when the person died. Insects can be useful to the criminalist in other ways. Some are only found in specific areas. So if those bugs are found on the windscreen or grille of a suspect's car, the entomologist will know where that car has recently been.

THE GOUFFE CASE

FRANCE, 1889. PARIS HAD BECOME EUROPE'S MOST MODERN CITY. FROM THE TOP OF THE NEWLY BUILT EIFFEL TOWER, A VISITOR COULD SEE WIDE, TREE-LINED BOULEVARDS STRETCHING BETWEEN GRAND AND ELEGANT BUILDINGS. TOURISTS FROM AROUND THE WORLD FLOCKED TO THE NEW CAPITAL CITY OF CULTURE.

ON THE EDGE OF THE CITY STOOD ANOTHER HIGH POINT, THE HILL OF MONTMARTRE. UNLIKE THE CITY CENTRE'S BROAD AVENUES, MONTMARTRE HAD KEPT ITS NARROW STREETS AND LANES AND WAS POPULAR WITH ARTISTS, WRITERS AND MUSICIANS. 49-YEAR-OLD TOUSSAINT AUGUSTIN GOUFFE, A LOCAL BAILIFF, WAS WELL KNOWN THERE. HE LIKED TO SPEND FRIDAY EVENINGS RELAXING IN THE HILL'S CAFES AND RESTAURANTS.

FRIDAY, 26 JULY, WAS NO DIFFERENT. AFTER CLOSING HIS OFFICE, THE BAILIFF MET WITH SOME OF HIS FRIENDS.

IS YOUR KNEE GIVING YOU TROUBLE AGAIN?

OOF! SLOW DOWN. I CAN'T WALK AS QUICKLY AS YOU TWO, REMEMBER.

THE WHOLE LEG ACHES TODAY.

WE'RE GOING TO THE MOULIN GALETTE FOR DINNER LATER ON. WHY DON'T YOU COME ALONG, TOUSSAINT?

I'D LIKE TO, BUT I ALREADY HAVE DINNER PLANS.

JUST AFTER SEVEN O'CLOCK GOUFFE SAID GOODBYE TO HIS FRIENDS AND LEFT THEM. THEY NEVER SAW HIM AGAIN.

SUNDAY, 28 JULY. INSPECTOR GORON AND HIS ASSISTANT, SERGEANT JAUME, WERE AT TOUSSAINT GOUFFE'S OFFICE IN THE RUE MONTMARTRE. HE HAD NOT BEEN SEEN SINCE FRIDAY AND THE POLICE WERE INVESTIGATING THE DISAPPEARANCE.

WELL, WHAT HAVE YOU FOUND, JAUME?

SOMEONE WAS HERE BEFORE US, SIR, THE ROOM'S BEEN SEARCHED. WHOEVER IT WAS DIDN'T FIND THIS, THOUGH.

THERE MUST BE THOUSANDS OF FRANCS HERE!

YES, 14,000 - I COUNTED THEM. IT WAS LYING UNDER A PILE OF PAPERS. THE INTRUDER MISSED IT.

HMM. THERE ARE BURNT MATCHES ON THE FLOOR. DID ANYONE SEE THE INTRUDER?

THE HALL PORTER HEARD SOMEONE COME UP THE STAIRS TO THE OFFICE AT AROUND NINE O'CLOCK.

HE THOUGHT IT WAS GOUFFE AT FIRST. WHEN THE INTRUDER LEFT A FEW MINUTES LATER, HE SAW THAT IT WASN'T.

DID THE PORTER SEE HIS FACE?

NO, IT WAS TOO DARK.

NEWS OF THE DISCOVERY REACHED INSPECTOR GORON. HE SENT JAUME AND GOUFFE'S BROTHER-IN-LAW TO IDENTIFY THE BODY.

GASP!

I SHOULD HAVE WARNED YOU. THEY DON'T LOOK SO PRETTY AFTER A FEW WEEKS OUTSIDE IN THIS HEAT.

OUTSIDE... TAKE A DEEP BREATH, SIR. YOU'LL FEEL BETTER IN A MINUTE OR TWO.

I'M SORRY, IT WAS A BIT OF A SHOCK. IT'S NOT MY BROTHER-IN-LAW. THAT - THING - HAS BLACK HAIR. TOUSSAINT'S IS BROWN.

BY THE AUTUMN, THE CASE SEEMED TO BE AT A DEAD END UNTIL, BY CHANCE, GORON MET ONE OF GOUFFE'S FRIENDS...

DON'T YOU THINK IT STRANGE THAT TWO PEOPLE FROM THE SAME PART OF PARIS SHOULD GO MISSING AT THE SAME TIME, INSPECTOR?

A 'SECOND' PERSON? WHO?

MICHEL EYRAUD WAS 46 YEARS OF AGE. EYRAUD'S BUSINESS HAD RECENTLY FAILED AND HE WAS THOUSANDS OF FRANCS IN DEBT. INSPECTOR GORON LEARNED THAT HE HAD LEFT PARIS THE DAY AFTER GOUFFE'S DISAPPEARANCE, ALONG WITH A FRIEND, 21-YEAR-OLD GABRIELLE BOMPARD.

SOON ANOTHER BREAKTHROUGH WAS MADE. A SMASHED TRUNK HAD BEEN FOUND IN THE SAME WOOD AS THE BODY. AT GARE DE LYON, PARIS – THE RAILWAY STATION THAT SERVED THE SOUTHEAST OF FRANCE...

THE POLICE IN LYON DIDN'T LINK THE TRUNK TO THE CRIME AT FIRST, JAUME. IT WAS FOUND NOWHERE NEAR THE BODY AND A RAILWAY LABEL ON IT WAS DATED '1888'.

THE DATE ON THE LABEL IS SMUDGED AND NOT EASY TO READ. BUT THEN A KEY FOUND CLOSE TO THE BODY FITTED THE TRUNK'S LOCK.

THE RAILWAY RECORDS OFFICE...

HERE IT IS! THE TRUNK, WEIGHING 230 POUNDS, WAS PUT ON A TRAIN BOUND FOR LYON...

...ON 27 JULY **1889**, THE DAY AFTER GOUFFE'S DISAPPEARANCE. THE BODY IN LYON IS FROM PARIS.

IN NOVEMBER INSPECTOR GORON WENT TO LYON AND HAD THE MYSTERY BODY DUG UP FROM ITS GRAVE.

HE HAD ARRANGED FOR DR LACASSAGNE FROM THE LYON SCHOOL OF FORENSIC MEDICINE TO PERFORM A NEW AUTOPSY.

DON'T YOU WANT TO GET A CLOSER LOOK, JAUME?

I'VE ALREADY SEEN ENOUGH OF THE BODY, SIR. BESIDES, IT'S LITTLE MORE THAN A SKELETON...

...WHAT CAN LACASSAGNE TELL US FROM THAT?

LOOKING AT THE PELVIS, I CAN SEE THAT IT IS MALE. THE FEMALE PELVIS IS SLIGHTLY WIDER.

LOOKING AT THE WEAR ON HIS TEETH, I WOULD SAY HE WAS BETWEEN 45 AND 50 YEARS OLD.

BY MEASURING THE THIGH AND UPPER ARM BONES I CAN TELL HOW TALL HE WAS.

IT STILL CAN'T BE GOUFFE, THOUGH. THE HAIR IS THE WRONG COLOUR.

THE HAIR HAS BEEN DYED. ITS REAL COLOUR IS BROWN.

REALLY? COULD YOU PASS ME THAT BOWL OF WATER, PLEASE?

I PRESENT TO YOU MR TOUSSAINT AUGUSTIN GOUFFE.

SO, WE KNOW WHO THE VICTIM IS. ALL WE HAVE TO DO NOW IS CONNECT THE TRUNK TO EYRAUD AND BOMPARD, AND WE'VE SOLVED THE CRIME.

BACK IN PARIS, GORON HAD A REPLICA OF THE TRUNK PUT ON DISPLAY. THE EFFORT PAID OFF. A HOTEL OWNER FROM LONDON WAS IN PARIS AT THE TIME...

I'VE SEEN THAT TRUNK BEFORE! I MUST LET THE POLICE KNOW.

HE REMEMBERED THAT A TRUNK, EXACTLY LIKE THE ONE ON SHOW, HAD BEEN BOUGHT IN ENGLAND BY A FRENCH COUPLE WHO WERE STAYING AT HIS HOTEL.

THEY WERE MICHEL EYRAUD AND GABRIELLE BOMPARD. WE HAVE THEM, JAUME!

WARRANTS FOR THEIR ARREST WERE ISSUED. BEFORE SHE COULD BE CAUGHT, BOMPARD GAVE HERSELF UP.

AH, INSPECTOR GORON, I UNDERSTAND YOU'RE LOOKING FOR ME.

SHE BLAMED EYRAUD FOR THE MURDER.

BUT INSPECTOR, YOU MUST BELIEVE ME, IT WAS ALL EYRAUD'S IDEA! HE TRICKED ME INTO HELPING HIM!

LOCK HER UP.

EYRAUD HAD FLED FROM FRANCE. IN JUNE 1890, HE WAS EVENTUALLY CAUGHT IN HAVANA, CUBA.

WHEN GORON CONFRONTED THE PAIR WITH THE EVIDENCE, THEY CONFESSED. AT LAST THE INSPECTOR KNEW THE WHOLE STORY.

THE KILLERS HAD CHOSEN GOUFFE CAREFULLY. EYRAUD WAS IN FINANCIAL TROUBLE AND KNEW THE BAILIFF CARRIED LARGE AMOUNTS OF MONEY AROUND WITH HIM.

BOMPARD HAD MADE FRIENDS WITH GOUFFE AND INVITED HIM TO HER APARTMENT...

AT ABOUT EIGHT O'CLOCK BOMPARD TOOK GOUFFE HOME WITH HER.

IS IT FAR, DEAR? ONLY - IT'S MY KNEE, YOU SEE...

NO, JUST A LITTLE FARTHER.

LATER...

WHY DON'T YOU SIT OVER THERE ON THE COUCH WHILE I GET SOME WINE?

THEY WERE NOT ALONE IN THE ROOM. MICHEL EYRAUD WAS ALSO THERE...

...HIDING.

GOUFFE WAS ENJOYING BOMPARD'S COMPANY.

A CURTAIN CORD TIE WOULD MAKE YOU LOOK SO HANDSOME, TOUSSAINT.

SUDDENLY...

NOW YOU'RE MAKING FUN OF ME, MISS BOMPARD.

IN A FLASH, EYRAUD HAD GRABBED THE CORD, TIED IT TO A ROPE AND PULLEY...

...AND HEAVED.

AFTER A FEW MINUTES GOUFFE WAS DEAD. THEY DID NOT KNOW THAT ON FRIDAYS, HE LEFT THE DAY'S TAKINGS IN HIS OFFICE.

IS THIS ALL THE MONEY HE HAD? 150 FRANCS*?

I DON'T UNDERSTAND. NORMALLY HE CARRIES THOUSANDS! IT MUST ALL BE AT HIS OFFICE.

*IN 1889 A COMMON LABOURER IN PARIS EARNED ABOUT FOUR FRANCS A DAY.

EYRAUD RUSHED TO GOUFFE'S OFFICE IN THE RUE MONTMARTRE.

HE HAD THE BAILIFF'S KEYS AND LET HIMSELF IN.

I CAN'T SEE A THING! I SHOULD HAVE BROUGHT CANDLES. I HAVE SOME MATCHES – THEY'LL HAVE TO DO.

WHEN HE HAD USED ALL HIS MATCHES, HE LEFT – WITHOUT FINDING THE HIDDEN 14,000 FRANCS.

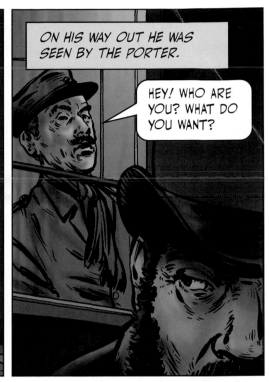

ON HIS WAY OUT HE WAS SEEN BY THE PORTER.

HEY! WHO ARE YOU? WHAT DO YOU WANT?

BACK AT THE APARTMENT...

IT'S TOO LATE TO TURN BACK NOW. WE HAVE TO STICK TO THE PLAN.

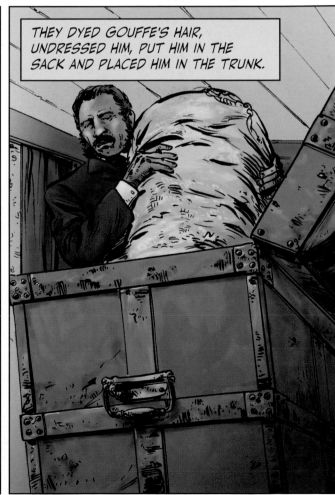

THEY DYED GOUFFE'S HAIR, UNDRESSED HIM, PUT HIM IN THE SACK AND PLACED HIM IN THE TRUNK.

THE FOLLOWING DAY THE KILLERS CAUGHT THE TRAIN TO LYON. IN A WOOD JUST OUTSIDE THE CITY...

EYRAUD TOOK THE TRUNK TO A DIFFERENT PART OF THE WOOD AND SMASHED IT SO THAT IT WOULD NOT BE CONNECTED TO THE CRIME. THE BODY WAS LEFT IN THE PLACE WHERE IT WAS FOUND TWO WEEKS LATER.

ON 16 DECEMBER 1890, THE TRIAL OF MICHEL EYRAUD AND GABRIELLE BOMPARD BEGAN. FIVE DAYS LATER IT WAS OVER. BOMPARD WAS SENTENCED TO 20 YEARS IN PRISON.

MICHEL EYRAUD, YOU HAVE BEEN FOUND GUILTY OF MURDER. THE SENTENCE OF THE COURT IS DEATH.

EARLY ON THE MORNING OF 3 FEBRUARY 1891, EYRAUD WAS TAKEN FROM HIS CELL IN LA ROQUETTE PRISON TO THE GUILLOTINE THAT STOOD OUTSIDE THE PRISON GATES.

LATER...

I STILL DON'T UNDERSTAND WHY THEY WENT ALL THE WAY TO LYON TO GET RID OF THE BODY.

FOR THE SAME REASON THEY WENT TO ENGLAND TO BUY THE TRUNK - BOTH PLACES ARE FAR FROM PARIS.

THEY THOUGHT THAT NEITHER THE BODY NOR THE TRUNK COULD BE TRACED HERE...

...AND WITHOUT A BODY WE COULDN'T PROVE A MURDER HAD BEEN COMMITTED. HAD WE NOT BEEN ABLE TO IDENTIFY GOUFFE, THEIR PLAN MIGHT HAVE SUCCEEDED.

IN 1903 GABRIELLE BOMPARD WAS RELEASED FROM PRISON. FOR A SHORT TIME SHE APPEARED ON THE PARIS STAGE IN A DRAMATIC RE-ENACTMENT OF THE MURDER. IT WAS NOT A SUCCESS.

THE END

23

BODY IN THE CARPET

10:30 PM, 21 SEPTEMBER 1986, INTERSTATE 95, GREENWICH, CONNECTICUT. THE POLICE HAD BEEN WAITING FOR THE MEDICAL EXAMINER TO ARRIVE. NOW THAT HE WAS THERE THEY COULD CONTINUE.

HAS ANYONE TOUCHED IT?

ONLY THE GUY WHO FOUND IT. THAT'S HOW WE KNOW THERE'S A BODY WRAPPED INSIDE.

IT'S FEMALE AND BEEN DEAD FOR SOME TIME, I'D SAY.

HELP ME UNROLL IT.

WE'RE NOT GOING TO GET A TIME OF DEATH OUT OF HER - SHE'S BEEN HERE TOO LONG TO USE THE NORMAL MARKERS. THIS IS ONE FOR THE BUG DETECTIVES.

MAGGOTS AND INSECTS WERE COLLECTED FROM THE BODY. SOME WERE KILLED, OTHERS WERE KEPT ALIVE.

THE SAMPLES WERE SENT TO DR WILLIAM KRINSKY AT YALE UNIVERSITY, NEW HAVEN, CONNECTICUT. MEANWHILE, THE POLICE HAD FOUND OUT THAT THE BODY BELONGED TO 26-YEAR-OLD SYLVIA HUNT. SHE HAD BEEN STABBED TO DEATH.

GOOD, THEY'VE SENT LIVE BLOWFLY MAGGOTS AND PUPAE*.

*SEE PAGE 29.

WHAT'S SO SPECIAL ABOUT BLOWFLIES? TO ME A FLY IS JUST A FLY.

THESE HAVE A VERY PREDICTABLE LIFE CYCLE, OFFICER.

WE KNOW HOW LONG EACH STAGE OF THEIR DEVELOPMENT TAKES.

25

DR KRINSKY PLACED BLOWFLY PUPAE FROM THE CRIME SCENE IN A HATCHING BOX AND KEPT IT AT 25°C.

THEY'RE USUALLY THE FIRST INSECT ON THE SCENE WHENEVER THERE'S A BODY AROUND.

WHEN THEY HATCH I'LL BE ABLE TO FIGURE OUT WHEN THE EGGS WERE LAID. THE BODY MUST HAVE DIED NOT LONG BEFORE THAT TIME.

AN ADULT BLOWFLY HAS AN EXCELLENT SENSE OF SMELL...

...AND CAN TRACK DOWN A CORPSE JUST MINUTES OLD.

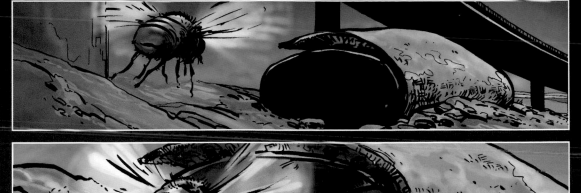

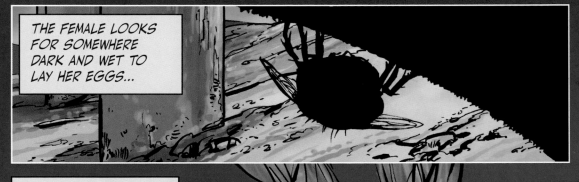

THE FEMALE LOOKS FOR SOMEWHERE DARK AND WET TO LAY HER EGGS...

...EITHER IN A NATURAL BODY OPENING...

...OR IN A FRESH WOUND.

THE EGGS HATCH IN LESS THAN A DAY.

OVER THE NEXT TWO DAYS THE MAGGOTS FEED ON THE DECAYING FLESH. THEY SHED THEIR SKIN TWICE, EACH TIME BECOMING LARGER.

AFTER EATING FOR SIX MORE DAYS, THE MAGGOTS CRAWL AWAY FROM THE BODY.

THEY BECOME SHORT AND FAT AS THEIR SKIN HARDENS AND THEY TURN INTO PUPAE.

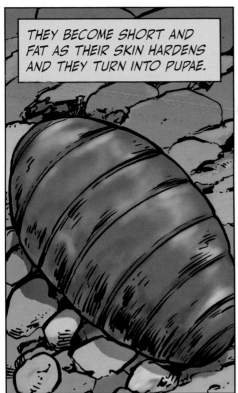

INSIDE ITS HARD CASE THE MAGGOT TAKES SIX DAYS TO CHANGE INTO AN ADULT BLOWFLY...

...AND THE CYCLE STARTS ALL OVER.

HOWEVER, WORKING OUT WHEN THE EGGS WERE LAID ISN'T ALWAYS EASY. SEVERAL THINGS HAVE TO BE TAKEN INTO ACCOUNT. FOR INSTANCE, TEMPERATURE HAS A GREAT EFFECT ON THEIR GROWTH RATE.

IT SLOWS DOWN IN COLD WEATHER, WHICH MEANS THAT THE EGGS MAY HAVE BEEN LAID EARLIER THAN FIRST THOUGHT.

SO I HAVE TO CHECK THE LOCAL WEATHER REPORTS TO SEE HOW WARM OR COLD IT'S BEEN.

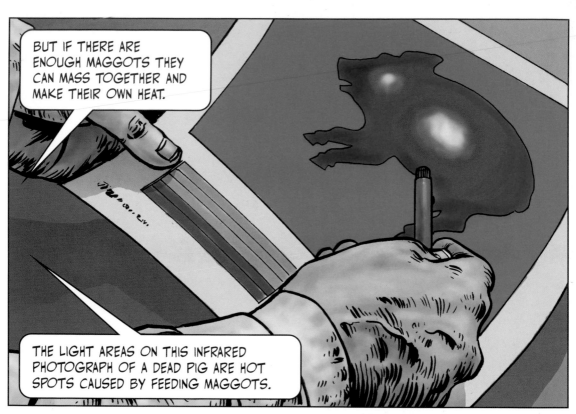

BUT IF THERE ARE ENOUGH MAGGOTS THEY CAN MASS TOGETHER AND MAKE THEIR OWN HEAT.

THE LIGHT AREAS ON THIS INFRARED PHOTOGRAPH OF A DEAD PIG ARE HOT SPOTS CAUSED BY FEEDING MAGGOTS.

THE GROWTH RATE CAN BE NORMAL EVEN WHEN IT'S COLD, SO I NEED TO KNOW HOW MANY MAGGOTS HAVE BEEN FEEDING ON A BODY.

FINDING THIS OUT CAN BE DIFFICULT AT TIMES. ANOTHER TYPE OF MAGGOT FEEDS ON BLOWFLY MAGGOTS, REDUCING THEIR NUMBER. COMING UP WITH A DATE FOR WHEN THE EGGS WERE LAID CAN TAKE SOME WORKING OUT!

AT 1:30 PM ON 25 SEPTEMBER, THE FIRST ADULT BLOWFLIES EMERGED. DR KRINSKY COULD NOW FIGURE OUT WHEN THE BLOWFLY EGGS WERE LAID.

STATE SUPERIOR COURT, STAMFORD, CONNECTICUT. IN AUGUST 1990, YURI HERNANDEZ WAS BROUGHT TO TRIAL FOR THE MURDER OF SYLVIA HUNT. DR KRINSKY GAVE HIS EVIDENCE.

THE FIRST BLOWFLY EGGS WOULD HAVE BEEN LAID ON THE BODY ON MONDAY MORNING, 15TH SEPTEMBER.

THE BODY OF SYLVIA HUNT WAS LEFT BY INTERSTATE 95 BEFORE SUNRISE ON 15TH SEPTEMBER.

THAT MEANS SYLVIA HUNT WAS MURDERED BEFORE THAT TIME AND DATE.

AT THE END OF AUGUST, HERNANDEZ WAS FOUND GUILTY OF MURDERING SYLVIA HUNT. DR KRINSKY'S EVIDENCE DID NOT PROVE THAT HERNANDEZ HAD KILLED HUNT, BUT IT DID GIVE AN APPROXIMATE TIME OF HER DEATH AND IT SHOWED THAT HERNANDEZ WAS IN GREENWICH WHEN THE MURDER WAS COMMITTED. THIS, COMBINED WITH OTHER EVIDENCE, WAS ENOUGH TO CONVICT HIM.

THE END

THE GASKET MAN

...THESE CASKETS AREN'T EMPTY.

THE LOCAL NEWS STATION SOON RAN THE STORY.

NO ONE KNOWS WHY THE BODIES WERE NOT BURIED. THE POLICE BELIEVE THE TWO MEN DIED OF NATURAL CAUSES AND ARE MORE CONCERNED WITH IDENTIFYING THEM FOR NOW.

THIS IS MARC SANTIA FOR WDIV TV-FOUR.

DO YOU THINK WE'LL EVER FIND OUT WHO THEY WERE?

NOT FROM THEIR FACES WE WON'T. YOU SAW WHAT THEY LOOK LIKE -THEY'RE TOO FAR GONE TO BE RECOGNISED.

'UNKNOWN MALE 142' WAS QUICKLY IDENTIFIED. LEONARD 'JUNIOR' SMITH HAD BEEN PUT IN HIS CASKET WEARING A BLUE JUMPSUIT. HIS FAMILY IDENTIFIED HIM FROM ITS DESCRIPTION.

MRS POPE TOLD US THAT UNCLE JUNIOR HAD BEEN CREMATED.

WE SHOULD HAVE KNOWN SOMETHING WAS WRONG WHEN WE NEVER GOT THE ASHES.

BY MARCH 2006, 'UNKNOWN MALE 141' WAS STILL UNCLAIMED AND LYING IN THE WAYNE COUNTY MORTUARY. MEDICAL EXAMINER G.T. JONES DECIDED TO CALL IN OUTSIDE HELP.

THE MICHIGAN STATE POLICE SENT ALONG TROOPER SARAH FOSTER, FORENSIC ARTIST.

I'LL GET SOME PHOTOGRAPHS OF HIM FIRST.

HERE HE IS. AS YOU CAN SEE, HE'S PRETTY SHRIVELLED UP.

AND THEN I'M GOING TO NEED THE HEAD.

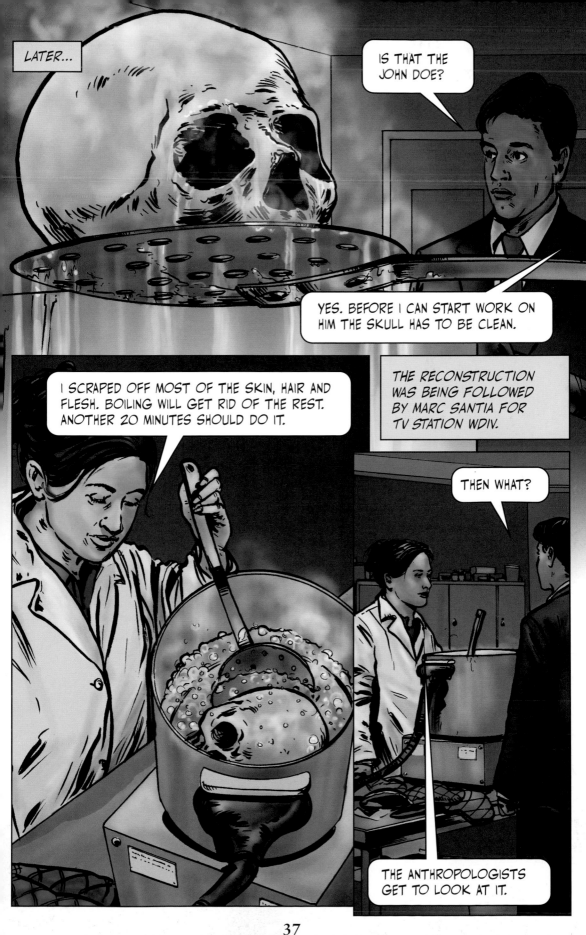

LATER...

IS THAT THE JOHN DOE?

YES. BEFORE I CAN START WORK ON HIM THE SKULL HAS TO BE CLEAN.

I SCRAPED OFF MOST OF THE SKIN, HAIR AND FLESH. BOILING WILL GET RID OF THE REST. ANOTHER 20 MINUTES SHOULD DO IT.

THE RECONSTRUCTION WAS BEING FOLLOWED BY MARC SANTIA FOR TV STATION WDIV.

THEN WHAT?

THE ANTHROPOLOGISTS GET TO LOOK AT IT.

WHEN THE SKULL WAS COMPLETELY CLEAN, SARAH FOSTER TOOK IT TO SHOW DR TODD FENTON AT THE MICHIGAN STATE UNIVERSITY ANTHROPOLOGY DEPARTMENT.

FROM THE SHAPE OF THE EYE SOCKETS AND THE NASAL OPENING I CAN SAY THAT HE WAS BLACK. HE WAS ALSO ELDERLY.

SARAH FOSTER'S STUDIO...

THE FIRST THING I HAVE TO DO IS SET THE JAW AT THE RIGHT ANGLE AND PROTECT THE FRAGILE BONES OF THE NOSE AND EYES WITH COTTON AND TAPE.

THESE CHARTS GIVE ME AN AVERAGE THICKNESS OF FAT AND MUSCLE AT VARIOUS POINTS ON THE SKULL.

I CUT PLASTIC DEPTH MARKER PEGS TO THE RIGHT LENGTH AND GLUE THEM IN PLACE.

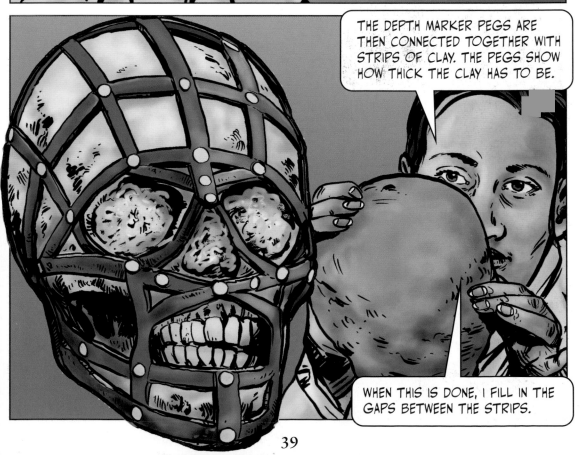

THE DEPTH MARKER PEGS ARE THEN CONNECTED TOGETHER WITH STRIPS OF CLAY. THE PEGS SHOW HOW THICK THE CLAY HAS TO BE.

WHEN THIS IS DONE, I FILL IN THE GAPS BETWEEN THE STRIPS.

THE RECONSTRUCTION BECOMES MORE ARTISTIC NOW. I START WITH THE MOUTH.

I CAN FIGURE OUT HOW BIG THE NOSE SHOULD BE BY MEASURING THE SMALL BONE HERE.

THE NOSE WILL STICK OUT THREE TIMES AS FAR.

AND IF I ADD EIGHT MILLIMETRES TO EITHER SIDE OF THE NASAL HOLE, THAT WILL GIVE ME THE WIDTH OF THE NOSE.

ONCE THE RECONSTRUCTION WAS FINISHED THE POLICE HAD FLYERS PRINTED. LATER, WDIV FEATURED THE STORY ON THE EVENING NEWS.

...BUT IF IT HELPS JOG SOMEONE'S MEMORY THEN IT'S BEEN A SUCCESS.

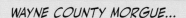
WAYNE COUNTY MORGUE...

EXCUSE ME, I'M HERE ABOUT THE BODY THAT WAS ON THE NEWS LAST NIGHT. I THINK IT'S MY BROTHER, JIMMY. I'VE GOT A PHOTOGRAPH OF HIM HERE.

HE LOOKS JUST LIKE THE MAN ON THE FLYER.

JIMMY LEE ADAMS HAD DIED IN FEBRUARY 2003, AGED 64, BUT DUE TO A MISUNDERSTANDING HE HAD NOT BEEN BURIED. WITHOUT THE SKILLS OF THE FORENSIC ARTIST, THE ADAMS FAMILY WOULD NEVER HAVE KNOWN WHAT HAD HAPPENED TO HIM.

THE END

INDEX

A

Adams, Jimmy Lee, 43

autopsy, 14

B

bailiff, 8–9, 17, 20

Bender, Frank, 45

Bompard, Gabrielle, 13, 16-18, 22-23

boulevard, 8

C

cartilage, 15

E

Eyraud, Michel, 13, 16-20, 22-23

F

Fenton, Dr Todd, 38

Flannery, Wanda, 45

forensic anthropologists, 6 7, 37-38, 44

forensic artists, 7, 36, 40, 43, 45

forensic entomologists, 4, 7, 44-45

forensic odontologists, 6

Foster, Sarah, 36, 38

G

Goron, Inspector, 10, 12-14, 16-17

Gouffé, Toussaint Augustin, 6, 8-13, 16-18, 20-21, 23

guillotine, 23

H

Hernandez, Yuri, 31

Hunt, Sylvia, 25, 31

I

intruder, 10

J

Jaume, Sergeant, 10, 12-14, 17

Jones, G. T., 36

K

Krinsky, Dr William, 25-26, 31

L

Lacassagne, Dr, 14

List, John Emil, 45

M

Maples, Dr William, 44

mortuary, 36

N

Nicholas II, Csar, 44

P

police, 4, 6, 10-11, 13, 16, 24-25, 32, 35-36, 44-45

Pope, Ellis, 32-33, 36

S

Santia, Marc, 35, 37

skeletons, 6-7, 14, 44

Smith, Leonard 'Junior', 36

Snow, Clyde, 44

T

thyroid, 15

V

vandalism, 32-33